Blooming Through The Darkness

A Collection of Poetry & Prose

Evangeline Barry

Illustrations and cover image done by Danielle George

WRITERS REPUBLIC L.L.C.
515 Summit Ave. Unit R1
Union City, NJ 07087, USA

Website: *www.writersrepublic.com*
Hotline: *1-877-656-6838*
Email: *info@writersrepublic.com*

Ordering Information:
Quantity sales. Special discounts are available on quantity purchases by corporations, associations, and others. For details, contact the publisher at the address above.

Library of Congress Control Number:		2022944710
ISBN-13:	979-8-88536-332-7	[Paperback Edition]
	979-8-88536-468-3	[Hardback Edition]
	979-8-88536-333-4	[Digital Edition]

Rev. date: 08/23/2022

For my Nana, you are the moon and the stars.
For my Papa, you are the sun and may you continue to
shine ever so brightly in heaven.

Prelude

I would like to start by thanking every single person who is reading this right now, thank you for deciding to add *Blooming Through The Darkness* to your reading list. I am beyond estatic and incredibly nervous to share this with all of you. When I fell back into my love for writing 7 years ago, my intention was not to write a book; it was not the goal. The goal was to use my writing to escape the dark place that I was in at that time. It took me a few years to mentally be in a better place and aside from God , writing saved me. This book is a combination of all the feelings, emotions, changes and experiences that I have been through over the past 8 years. I love helping people in any way that I can and I wrote this book with hopes that it would resonate with anyone who has felt what I have. Just know that you are not alone in anything that you are going through and every experience brings an opportunity to grow in different ways. Thank you to everyone that encouraged me to write this book and pushed me to finish it. It was not easy allowing myself to be completely vulnerable and honest with myself while working on this but I am glad that I was able to do so and I feel a special type of freedom.

Trigger Warning

Please be advised that this book contains material on anxiety, alcohol/drug use, death, depression, emotional abuse, self-harm, suicidal ideation, suicide, trauma, racial issues and other mental health related issues. If you feel triggered in any way while reading , please take care of yourself and reach out to anyone that you trust or get in touch with resources that are available to you such as hot-lines, medical professionals etc.

Heartbreak and Rebounds

Winter Pain

As the snow accumulates, I think of how tightly bonded we once were. When the snow melts away in a few days, I think of how we disintegrated the same way.

Lonely Clouds

I am sorry that you were not ready for all that I am and all that I am about to become.
I needed to heal and so did you but instead of working on you, you decided to look for an escape in someone else.

Sometimes I wonder if I even knew you as well as I thought I did.
I have been lied to a lot in my life but somehow when you lied to me, it was like the sun betrayed the sky and left the clouds to dance alone in the sky.

Broken in Every Way

I swear I cannot seem to find any authenticity and genuineness in
this situation.
Maybe, I am quick to question this relationship because I am still
holding onto feelings that come and go.
I am curious to know what is going on behind those walls since none
of this makes sense to me.
It is hard to accept the fact that you lied to me and I am still awaiting
answers to questions that are not even relevant anymore.

When I see you with her, my chest still tightens, and my blood runs
cold.
Even though the love we had for each other has expired in your
mind, it has not expired in mine.
They say everyone is replaceable, but I always thought that I always
had a special place in your heart and that you would never forget
about me.
I just want someone to make me forget about you forever because
my heart breaks over and over every time I think about you loving
someone else.

Thought You Were The One

If you reached out to me a year from today, something must have possessed you to speak to me after everything that happened between us.

I would have to make a decision to either entertain the interaction and to be civil or not even entertain it at all.

This has happened too many times to count.

My heart always became softer than usual when you were involved.

I have been asked if I would go back to you if you wanted me to; as tempting as it would be and a small part of me wants it, I would be disrespecting myself if I did.

I would be saying that the way you treated me was okay.

The things that you said about me and even the way you spoke about me to others; I would be saying all of that was okay.

I would be saying it was okay for you to not be there for me when I needed you the most.

Okay for you to make me feel like I was too difficult of a person to even try.

It was like back and forth emotional abuse without me even realizing it.

All the good things you did for me, unfortunately got drowned by the bad you turned out to be.

We both had our hands to blame for why a civil interaction could not work.

If you came back a year from today, it would take a miracle for me to stupidly run back into your arms again.

Past Tense

I remember when we first met.
You were.. different, let's just put it that way.
Different has always been attractive to me.
There was a deep tingling inside my soul anytime I spoke to you or of you.
Your name was a frequently used word in my dictionary.
The dark clouds that were circling around me just decided to disappear when they saw you.

I was so sure that you were meant for me; then life happened over and over again.
We don't talk anymore.
I tried very hard.
You said you tried but you weren't trying as hard as I thought.

What a Damn Weakness

A mother always knows.
Do you know that saying
In this case my Nana always knows.
She knows and she has seen that my weakness is you.
That crushes me the most.
Being completely vulnerable with you was a risk.
Placing complete trust in you again was an even bigger risk.
That risk turned into a gun that shot me in the heart once we parted ways.
Nana always knows, right?
I'm pretty sure she thought we were exclusive and I can understand why.
She must've seen the way I looked at you.
I used all the energy and light in my body to look at you.
By the time I was done my soul was drained as I waited for you to restore it.

Wrong

I think about all of those times you scrutinized me for how I felt.
Those times you told me I don't understand or I'm thinking about
no one but myself.
Those times you made me feel like shit because you always wanted
to be right and I wouldn't let you.
I realized that you simply heard me but stopped listening.
You gave up as soon as I said something you didn't want to hear.
YOU are the one that doesn't understand.
I will never allow you to taint my reputation or invalidate how I feel
ever...again.

A Storm is Brewing

It all ends the same but the story behind how it all started will break you into pieces.

Not So Virgin Thighs.

I have not so virgin thighs because my thighs have wrapped around necks while my body has been rocked back and forth. I used to see sex as something sacred; a luxury of exploring my body that should only be given to certain people. However, this was before I knew what it felt like to feel pain that didn't make me feel like I wanted to die. The kissing, the rubbing of my skin against the other, the goosebumps I feel when he uses his hands to caress and squeeze. I feel chills up and down my spine when he opens me. Sex makes me enjoy being vulnerable under the sheets. During sex I feel like the other person is completely mines even though to them it's just sex and nothing more than that. The level of intimacy involved is enough for me to get high without trees and it's more than enough for me to feel intoxicated without the alcohol. You can't fake that much passion; at least that's what I thought in the beginning but then I started making rounds and exploring different bodies. In some cases, I did fake the passion because once I got what I wanted, my void was filled for at least a week.

I loved the man that made my thighs not so virgin. I loved him deeper than how deep I let him inside of me. Even though the action wasn't as intense as the other times after him, it was still filled with so much passion that I would never forget it as much as I want that memory to be erased. After him, I started searching for that passion elsewhere or even something close to it. No one ever came close.... yet. One thing I know for sure is that as much as he said he wanted to move on from that time where he loved me insanely. There's no way he will ever be able to forget when I sat on his lap and spoke butterflies in his ear, gave him chills when I went down and made him feel like the only man on this earth.

Not a Vacation

Men saw a vacation when they looked at her.

They treated her body as an escape.

A beautiful escape.

Only the brave ones stayed and took the 'risk' in exploring the lands beneath her body.

The ones filled with fear left because this is a vacation and not a permanent destination.

They continued on with their journey to rinse and repeat with someone else.

Time To Bury You

Line his coffin with your broken blood vessels.
Dig a hole that's big enough to fit all the mistakes he made
with you.
Bury him with all the pain he caused you.

Broken Promise

Under the stars, you and I talked about taking on the world together.
We counted each star and named one thing that we loved about each other.
You held my hand tightly and promised that you will always be with me no matter the distance.

As time went by, those stars no longer meant something to you because when we grew apart and you were the one to give up first.
You lost all the love you had for me when things got difficult.
No one said that this was going to be easy.

Betrayal and Pain

15

The Hard Truth

The sun beamed on my face.
Your love shined in my veins.
Until I saw a glimpse of the future and you weren't in it.
I was hopeful but not naive.
I prayed for things to not change.

But then, I realized that things had to change for me to evolve.
I had to acknowledge all the good things that you saw in me but
I had to see it on my own.
You had to change for me to see my worth and find strength
within myself.
I had to grow up and leave the fantasy of us behind me but I've
never forgotten about us.
My evolution wasn't going to have enough space in your heart
and I had to be okay with that.

Unexpected Goodbye

It's impossible to not miss you after all the memories we've shared.
It's hard to not think that it wasn't real.
It's hard to accept that you didn't want to be around anymore.
No explanation and no proper goodbye.
It's hard to not blame myself every day.
I'm swimming in an ocean of different reasons why you wouldn't want to go on long walks with me anymore.

We have been through so much , so damn much and you assured me that you would always be here.
I thought our friendship was strong and I thought our communication skills was even stronger.
But apparently not; it's hard to let you go knowing that I would never have closure.
It's even harder to take out this knife in my back without my blood running out.

Archived but Not Forgotten

I need to let go but I'm not sure how.
It's been over a year since you decided that I no longer deserved to
be a part of your life anymore.
For a reason that is still unknown to me.
It seems like much longer than a year and with all this free time in
isolation , you have crossed my mind at least once each week.
I wonder if you're okay.
There's no point in reaching out because I know that's not what
you want.

I want to stop caring about you.
I want to pretend like the friendship we had meant nothing to
me.
The same way it seemed to have meant nothing to you.
I'm too full of emotion to be heartless and I'm too sick of thinking
about you.
Even though I'm still heartbroken and will be for a long time; I
still pray for you.
Especially at a time like this.

Misled

We can either become products of our environment or shape and create our own environment to reflect the change that we want to be. It may be hard to do this sometimes if you're around negativity all the time. How do you work around it when you have to live with it ? Kia asked herself this question for most of her life. It seemed impossible to do without conflict arising. Kia was an outsider looking in and observing the relationship her boyfriend has with his mother." I'm worried for him to be really honest." Kia said to her friend Lisa . " It's one thing to treat me like shit but it's another thing to project all that toxicity onto your own son... I just don't understand it. Lisa chimed in , " When you told me what she said to you, I almost didn't believe it. Considering that she showed you so much love at first." Kia couldn't believe it either. She was constantly a victim of emotional abuse and that's one of the reasons she never wanted to live with her own mother. Kia was madly in love with her boyfriend Raheem and she was beginning to see all his underlying issues and connected the dots back to his mother.

Raheem's mother was not a bad person , she just wasn't mindful of what her hurtful words could do to people. She had alot of baggage and she saw Kia as a threat. She saw Kia as a young woman who could potentially take her son away, even though that was far from the truth but it seemed like Raheem's mother created illusions in her mind and convinced herself that it was all true.Raheem is aware of how difficult his mother can be however he can't do anything to change his mother but he knows that he can respond differently. Kia was determined not to let his mother get into her head but it was becoming harder each day.

Kia sat with Raheem one day and said. " I did everything to please her and she told me that I wasn't apart of her family. What's going to happen if we get married and have children ? Would she consider her grandchildren not part of her family just because they came from me?" Raheem shook his head , " That's pretty messed up. I don't think she realizes that she's sabotaging her own relationship with me by being terrible towards you." Kia looked to the sky and closed her eyes and all she could hope for is a family with Raheem and a chance for him to break this dysfunctional cycle from which he came. She just wanted the best for him because he deserves everything good.

Conflicted by Blood

The feeling of guilt as I stand by the intentions of my actions can be quite the storm of confliction.

That strange and uncomfortable feeling.

A healing transformation was happening within me and that's why I couldn't be a part of your journey.

There was hurt so deep and high levels of frustration.

 I couldn't unwrap myself from all of it and be what you wanted me to be.

Son of a Dragon

I feel terrible when I see the worry lines on your forehead because of the dragon never being pleased.
Being the child of a dragon must be hard .
Especially if one day the dragon did everything to protect you and then the next day she wouldn't help you with your broken wing.

What if Humans Were Different

Invalidation of my fears and pains will always hurt me.
It hurts more when it comes from the people you trust with your
intense thoughts.
Their intentions aren't always vile and the timing isn't always right.
I still lay here a w a k e thinking ; what would it be like if everyone
took a crash course in empathy?
I would have more reassurance when trust and humans are involved
that's for sure.

Bitter Betrayal

What happens when blood no longer seems to be thicker than water?
Broken hearts and sadness.
Sadness because your kindness and love was abused and questioned?
How could someone choose their friends over their family?
How could they let someone else dictate what they do and how they do it?
When will you realize what you did wrong?
I ask myself these questions everytime I think of you.
Everytime I think if I should have been a bigger person from the beginning and put a stop to the virus before it started.

I never hated you and I never will but I question what you think of me and why.
We all have internal demons that blind our judgement and cause us to turn against the people who only want to help us.
But I never thought they would push you to treat me the way you did.
Family shouldn't treat family like enemies.
Family shouldn't turn their backs on one another either; unless the relationship becomes morally unhealthy.
I needed the space to get back to me and to think about what I should say or shouldn't say.
I've been through this so many times before that I got tired of having to fix things that were never my fault to begin with.
I was always there and always had the patience.
But that never seemed like enough.

Battling with Pain

Accepting pain should never be an option.

Pain should never be able to swallow you whole or break your knees.

I wish I believed these words as clearly as I speak them.

But it takes time to perfectly practice what you preach.

So , forgive yourself when you feel like a fraud because we all feel just the same.

Advil

Imagine if there were pain relievers that relieved emotional pain.
Actual pills that helped that chest pain that you felt from seeing that
one person leave.
The chest pain that you felt but in reality it isn't actually there.
I think most of us , if not all of us; would be able to get through our
days with two advils for emotional pain.
Whether I pretend or not, these pills will diminish all the painful
memories I carry with me.

A Complicated Concept

People.

What are we? Who are we? Why are we who we are?

I've been on the earth for only 22 years and I have had so many different experiences with people and it has changed who I am in many different ways.

People never truly mean what they say, at least not everyone that you will meet. Sometimes I wish people were just genuine and not temporary or just frauds. They make me feel like they would be around...always.

But when I turned around looking for them after I'd climbed the mountain, they were no longer there. The love and care I show for people portrays the love and care that I always wished I received from day 1.

People are heartbreakers and don't try to convince me otherwise.

But why are we like this? When did we become less and less considerate of someone else's emotions and feelings?

When did we start disregarding what our loved ones have done for us?

When did I start seeing less good in people and more of the ugly truth?

I have become unsure of when the sun will rise and when will the solid snow melt into an ocean of my tears.

You don't see clarity in my tears or the love in my heart and I am exhausted from trying to make you see it.

People.

Some of them leave us breathless and some make us comfortable enough so that we lay our heads down and fall into their arms. Falling into their arms makes it easier for them to open our hearts just so that they could stab it and watch as life leaves within us.

Depression and The Whole Nine Yards

No Pedicure Can Fix This

You know things are bad when you rather use nail polish remover
to remove the ugly pain.
Maybe this will work because I'm so sick and tired of my
depression slowly removing my soul.

Losing

We are confused but also trying to find ourselves at the same time.
We may not believe in ourselves because there's no one to believe
in us.
We struggle in our own ways trying to make a path for ourselves.
We try to survive.
Staying positive is exhausting sometimes.
I'm always low on faith and hope.

God is always testing me and I always feel like I'm failing.
I stare into space with blank stares on my face.
I don't know what tomorrow will bring; that is a worry within
itself.
I always pace myself for the next disaster that would take another
piece of me.

A Dark Garden of Eden

Broken petals are under the bushes.
Broken clouds are in the sky.
They look undeniably beautiful despite their brokenness.
But when does broken start showing on the outside and when
does it affect what you look like?
Can you see it in my eyes ?
The blank and tired stare.
Can you see it on my lips?
A permanent frown that points towards hell; struggling to get to
heaven.

Fist Fighting with my Heart

I have a heart.
It keeps growing without my permission.
Sometimes, it interferes with the functions and the nerves in my brain.
My heart causes me to get emotionally opinionated in situations where there is cause for concern.
It's not always a good thing ...trust me.
Big hearts get physically assaulted from time to time.

My brain tells me to protect my heart when it starts to beat uncontrollably fast.
BA-BOM BA- BOM BA-BOM
Can't you hear it ? Says my brain.
Can you feel it ? Says the pain in my chest.
It's telling me to take a deep breath and gather my thoughts.
Inhale....exhale...
There's alot of things that are out of your control at this point.

What is done is done.
What was said was said for a reason.
What was mistaken has been recognized.
My brain told my heart that it needs to stop fuming over the actions of others.
It may be stupid and it may be annoying but nothing can be done on my part.
There's only soo much my body can take as a whole.
Breathe... again ... again ...
And while you're at it just walk away.

My Version of Hell

I wish I could make my insecurities disappear but instead of
trying to figure out how to deal with it on a daily basis, I've been
trying to bury them within the deepest depths of my soul.
When forced to face what truly lurks inside my mind; it makes
me sick. It makes me question my existence.
Some days are definitely harder than some.
People and situations make it better or worse.
I still try to stand behind a lot of my feelings and behaviour
because there's a deep reason behind it and I just wish people
would understand that.
Maybe life isn't as bad as it seems and I know that other people
have it worse than me but sometimes the definition of hell can
look like different things to different people.

Suicidal Intentions

Somehow, God giving me another chance to live warms my heart even though my body is so cold.

God gave us one another so that we can look after each other.

But somehow; I felt so defeated by life that it seemed much easier to descend with the sunset than live till morning to see the sun come up.

Tired

It's becoming harder to breathe and even harder to get up
after every defeat.

Anything she does never seems to be enough and she feels
unheard.

Everything is becoming too much and all she could do is curl
into a ball and cry silently.

At least that way , she won't bother anyone with her tears.

I'm Sorry

I avoid you because it hurts me more to hear the disappointment and concern in your voice.

It hurts me more to hear you say that you don't understand.

You're probably thinking that you raised me better or maybe you think that somewhere along the way , you missed something.

It hurts me that I hurt you, all I ever wanted was to make you proud.

You gave me everything and tried to fill those empty voids in my little body.

I just want you to know that it's not your fault and I promise you that I will get better.

Maybe not now, not tomorrow and not next week.

But someday I will be a better me.

Insomnia

Sleeping no longer became a safe haven.
The far away planets I made up in my head, no longer
became a resting place because I was too afraid to close my eyes.
Closing my eyes while inhaling and exhaling a hundred disheartening
emotions, would leave room for my demons to take over my resting
place.

My demons would parade on my planet and make a mockery of my
progress, my existence and my invisibility at the same time.
They would abuse and shatter my poor heart just a little bit more
as though it hasn't been through enough already.

Partly Cloudy with Red Skies

The day before yesterday and the day before that; the sky was red.
The sky was red because my heart was filled with anguish and pain.
There were no clouds.
   No birds.
   No planes.
Today it's partly cloudy with blue skies.
I don't feel completely better and it would be a while before I do but just like the skies are always changing, I know my life can change too.

My Anxiety Can Do Tricks

Taking public transportation is tiring and nerve-wrecking.
I always think of the million eyes that could be looking at me.
What does my face look like?
It looked fine when I was at home getting ready but who knows
what the atmosphere could've done to my pores.

I hate when people and their belongings touch me while I try to
drown their voices in my head with a little R&B or soul.
I play with my hands a million times and maybe if I continue to
stare at my shoes, I just might disappear.

The Club for Big Hearts

People with the biggest hearts have the most hardships.

We have the most 'support' systems that break down.

We've been in the most complicated situations with the most ignorant people.

We've been the mat at the doorstep for everyone to dust their dirty shoes on.

We've been the light for someone else but sometimes never for ourselves.

Having a big heart is such a heavy thing to carry around.

Sometimes I put her on the seat next to me on the train because she gets way too heavy.

Sometimes I also lock her away for awhile because feeling less than what I feel everyday is a relief... sometimes.

Distressed Damsel

That day , I strolled in the rain with no umbrella because the pouring droplets from the sky felt so comforting.
I needed comfort for my heavy heart.
Comfort from nature that was silent yet gentle.
I needed time to walk in the rain to figure out why my brain didn't want to turn off.
I never figured it out.

I felt heavy and bruised , bruises caused by my inner self.
Part of me was ruining my life.
Part of me wanted to be content with the blessings I still had.
Part of me just wanted to end every single voice in my head once and for all.
Part of me never wanted to hurt anyone the way I did.
Part of me was jealous of alot of things around me and part of me couldn't control it.

I felt disconnected with you and everyone else.
I felt like my body was drowning in more water than I was swimming in while in the womb.
Part of me thinks that you're tired of me.
Part of me believes you when you say you aren't.
Part of me tries to not feel hurt when they socialize with others and not me.
When I was always there for ...everyone.

I try to be there for me but ME doesn't understand why ME feels like this.

 I try to think about what things would have been like if my beginning was smoother than how it started.

My therapist told me that she told someone that I have been so strong considering what I went through.

She said that I still try to figure out where things went wrong and try to fix it.

She said that anything positive she says probably won't make a difference in how I look at myself.

It won't make the struggles go away.

All of this is nice to hear but I just wish that strong woman that everyone is talking about would look back at me in the mirror.

Going Fishin'

If I sit long enough in the deep waters, the waves would take me
10ft under.
Maybe I would be at peace then.

A Thought During Quarantine

Everyday brings a new emotion to process.
A new emotion to help combat its anxiety.
A new emotion of uncertainty.
I hate what our world has come to and I hate the way people play with death the same way they play with fire.
For once, we are all the same and we are all in need of the same things and we all need it severely.
However, the need that we should all desperately get down on our knees and pray for is God's mercy.

A Valid Question

How do I regulate my feelings without allowing myself to be
sucked into a hole of despair?
I've been searching for the answer for years.

The Stories In our Clothing

Clothing helps us express ourselves in the most extraordinary ways.
Clothing can represent different milestones in our life like a wedding
dress or a graduation gown.
I think pieces of clothing carry memories and some of those memories
can turn into triggers.
I remember when I wore that dress with the flowers and off the
shoulder sleeves, you deflowered me in that dress.
I can wash it a million times but I still smell your scent on it.
I remember when I wore that jean jacket when I met your family.
Your mother gushed at the fact that me and her were twinning with our
jackets.
I wore that gray hoodie with the graphics when I was about to get on
that plane and leave the only place I could call home.
I still feel the tears that fell on my ankle cut jeans that I wore that day.
I remember the long flowy black & white dress I wore to my cousin's
funeral.
I wore that dress too many times and I can still feel it drag on the road
as we walked behind his coffin.
I remember the rhinestone heels that I wore to my fifth form
graduation.
Heels were never my thing but the occasion forced me to wear them.
You were right behind me to catch me when I almost fell in those heels.
Update; I .never.wore .those. heels .again.
You see all my clothes and shoes have a story attached to them , some
will make you cry and some will make you laugh.
Slowly but surely, I have to make new and happy memories to replace
the ones that trigger me in these beautiful pieces of clothing that
express who I am perfectly.

Dying and Death

Time is Ticking

You're still here.
Maybe I shouldn't be sad and cry.
You're still alive and breathing but you're in pain.
A pain that is manageable on some days but on other days;
You
   want
      the
         pain
            to
               stop
                  for
                     good.

The fact that you can tell me that you've already accepted that
this pain won't last forever makes me somber.
Maybe today, or tomorrow ; or next week your pain will
resign to its slumber.
I'm prepared for today but not tomorrow.

06 /26/ 2018

I remember when I was 5, you tried to comb my hair for
school.
I bought the comb, the ribbons and the products for you in
your room.
I told you , " Do it the way Nana does it."
You grumbled at how complicated this task was about to be
but you tried.
My hair wasn't perfect afterwards but you still tried.
You're one of the first people that showed me what trying
looks like.
That's what I loved about you the most.

Empty

I keep looking to the sky; searching for you to tell me something wise.
For some reason I can't feel you at all.
I don't even have dreams about you.
It's just darkness and it feels like I've lost a part of my soul that can never
be replaced.

Your Ascension

I've been having flashbacks of your final destination lately.
When they rolled your wooden bed into the church ; I saw you laying there, soo frail and motionless.
My limbs turned into water and all I could was kneel down next to you.
Just like when I was little and you would have to bend or kneel to reach my level.
When I touched your arm one last time, I whispered , " T

         r

      a

        v

      e

   l

       safely and please let me know

when you get there.

Summer Mourning

It felt unreal seeing you lay there so still and not breathing.

No more breathing meant no more talking.

Not hearing your voice anymore meant I would stop laughing.

I would laugh at other things that people said and did but it wouldn't be the same.

It was selfish of me to think that this illness would just disappear.

It was selfish of me to think that you would want to continue living with compromised independence.

That day, the sun and the rain took turns to mourn you and I accepted it .

Until We Meet Again

I wonder what it feels like to become one with the clouds.

To live everlastingly in every sunrise and sunset.

It must feel refreshing to become part of such a breathtaking picture.

Tell me what it feels like to have a natural purpose in the next.

I wish it was possible to transform myself as part of the sky, just for a day.

I would love to touch your face again but I know it's not time yet.

Paralyzed by Grief

As time goes by, trying to walk without limbs is becoming harder.
Just like living without you is becoming harder.
Is my heart supposed to hurt even more each day ?
Isn't it supposed to get easier with time?

I wish I didn't have to wake up each morning and tell the walls in
my bedroom all the things that I wanted to tell you if you were still
here.
I know that you can hear me every morning and every night.
There isn't anything I wouldn't do to hear your voice again.

Papa's Interlude

You were right.
The world and the people in it aren't as good as they seem.
Anytime my mind is weary and my chest is tight , you appear.
You appear to tell me to merge the wants of my heart with the
truths that I refuse to see and decide who I want to be and what I
will not stand for.

Warmth in the Winter

You were made with the warmth of the sun and the fresh waters
of the beach.
Your laugh was filled with marketplace vibes.
Your skin resembled the sweetest molasses you could find.
You were made with the warmth of the sun and yet I can feel
your presence in this bitter cold air.

Road Trip

Acres of open fields and large old- fashioned houses with fine details to take your breath away.
Peace and quiet that doesn't make you feel lonely or restless.
I went on a road trip and it was refreshing to see the things that reminded me of home.
It wasn't exactly the same but it was close to it.

I never realized how anxious and distressed the city made me feel until I inhaled a new scenery.
This small town made everything look less depressing and more refreshing.
The one thing that caught my eye the most was two funeral homes that I saw.
I'm not a big fan of death or the factors around it but these funeral homes looked so beautiful on the outside.
Brightly painted in yellow and gold with white bars creating the welcoming porch and balcony.

Death can be devastating for almost anyone and it can bring up so many emotions that are hard to explain.
I consider funeral homes to be the last stop on earth for the dead so I guess making this environment beautiful in all forms is the best way to ease some of the pain.

Spiritual Presence

You are here with me.
In my lungs and in my heart.
I will live for you.

2 Years Later

It's only been two years but it feels like just yesterday.

It feels like just yesterday you got chosen to be an angel for the rest of us.

I've accepted that you aren't coming back and that this was for a higher purpose.

I'm still trying to make you proud every single day and I would never stop for as long as I shall live.

Joys and Sorrows Of Love

The First Time

That day, I was nervous and had no idea what to expect and what not to expect. To make me more on edge, I was already having a bad day and I had a lot on my mind. Usually I always had negative thoughts in the back of my mind when meeting a new guy or even the idea of dating. I just had too many bad experiences which is why I wasn't very hopeful about these situations. As I carefully applied my makeup and made sure each curl in my hair was full of bounce; I thought, would he even like me? I was finally ready and running a half an hour late. I called an Uber and went outside to meet the driver, as I sat in the car my hands were sweating and my heart was racing. This guy and I have been speaking for maybe little over a week and I was about to meet him for the first time. I knew for sure I was attracted to him, but I just didn't know what to expect when I saw him.
I got to the mall and he was already there but he went to an ATM so I sat in front of a coffee shop and waited for him to meet me. I scrolled through my phone as I waited, and I noticed from my peripheral vision; someone familiar walking towards me. I looked up and I felt an instant rush through my body and it felt weird, it was a feeling I haven't had in a long time. He was more beautiful in person and I felt a connection with him instantly. It just all seemed right in that very moment.

A Wild Summer Memory

The hot air and the beaming sun lured us outside to play.
Shorts and a crop top with flannel tied around my waist
seemed to be the best attire for this day.
As for you , you made the heat rise in the air but cooled my
body down with one look and a touch.
We went on an adventure that day and I never felt more free.
 It felt like the sun and the sweat from the sweltering hot day
brought us closer together.

Walking through trails , climbing steep little hills and
watching the sky reflect off of your eyes.
My feet ached and felt blistered but it didn't compare to the
pain I felt inside.
The pain that comes with mourning a loss and the pain of
getting on that plane in a few days to face the loss.
You made the day less gloomy and more delightful.
You made me see some sun between the stormy clouds in my
mind.

You will always feel like home when you remind me of the
little things that made up the childhoods that we had.
Those little things that only you and I could understand.
I hate the heat in Toronto sometimes, so humid and so hard to
breathe.
But when I'm with you I could feel the breeze on Maracas
beach.
You're like the cool and crisp breeze that circulates throughout
our little island and makes it easier for me to breathe.

Natural effects of your love

My love for you is like a daffodil that blooms in the middle of winter.
Even though winter brings out the worst in me , I somehow rise to love you everyday.
That smile of yours has been melting the ice that lingers in my heart from time to time.
When you reach for my hand and hold it gently, it keeps me warm everytime.

An Unlikely Mate

From Maroon 5's *'Never Gonna Leave This Bed'* to
Miguel's *'Sure Thing'*.
The music sounds sweeter and more of the truth
with you next to me.
I find comfort and safety in bed with you.
Our bed is where you come back to me on late nights
and assure me that you're sorry.
Assure me that you aren't going anywhere.

No matter how far I push you sometimes.
I knew from the start that we would have to
work hard for us.
I knew from the start that you were the one and that I
would be willing to fight for you.
You are the opposite of what I imagined my soulmate
would be but you balance my scale.
You balance me out so well and that's not an
easy thing to do.
You're my sure thing and my scale can't live
without you.

Lovesick

Overly ecstatic
So overjoyed that my cheeks become warm when
I hear your name.
Your hugs and kisses awakens my pores and your
smile is as bright as the sun can get.
Overly ecstatic to say that you're mine.
You are the best addition to this chapter and I hope you
make it to the end.

A Freeze in Time

Earth and the rest of planets stop spinning around the sun when your lips melt into mines. Everything around us seems to be a blur but all I can see clearly is you.

Honeymoon Garden

Nights when the moon is full and the air is cool but not
chilly.
Maybe on a half empty beach, I can lie on your chest and we
can talk about why people think they have to do everything
to impress their friends.
We can talk about why *Sunday Morning* by Maroon 5 is still a
necessary concept after all these years.
I can tell you about how living here became a little less
scarier when you came around.
Nights when the moon is full, I see the future and it's with
you.

When We Disagree

Sweeter than a mango once we get along.
Saltier than a saltfish if you do me wrong.
I will cry when I want to and I don't care what you say.
You don't seem to take me seriously and that's making me feel a
type of way.

When We Love

You take the time to learn my soul.
You have patience with my complex but soft heart.
Doing all the right things to satisfy my needs inside and out.
Bringing butterflies to my garden of flowers.
Inviting the ocean to collide with the shores of my mouth.
You are such a rare find and I'm glad that you're all mine.

Open

Let's blend our bodies together and create a milky way.
I miss you more than I did yesterday so come here and take my
breath away.

Confused

This love will make me go on tippy toes and reach for the sky.
This love will make me think hard after fights with you..

The See-Saw on Our Blood Vessels

Every other week we go to the playground.
Things were always fun and you came up with a new way to go
down the slides each time.
But then you got comfortable with me pushing you on the swing
, every other week.
I loved pushing you but sometimes I wanted to see what the sky
looked like from up there to.

The park got dismal and soon enough you didn't want to go to
the park anymore.
I wondered if you forgot how happy this made our souls.
The park helped us to hold each other's hand as tightly as we did
when we first met.

A new feeling of love and hope filled my strawberry shaped
heart, every time I see you.
I'm concerned because I don't see that glossy gaze when you look
at me.
I felt like so much more than I thought I was , the first time you
looked at me.

Love is Never Perfect

We've been through so much so quickly and we always recovered
but sometimes the same things keep coming up.
I only have control over myself and not you and maybe I hold on
so tightly because I'm afraid of you leaving.
You've told me so many times that you will never leave, you've
tried so hard to make up for times you failed me.

I've said sorry a million times for my difficult behaviour and you've
forgiven me a million times to match.
I've never met someone who fights for me as hard as you do and
even though we have our differences we are always willing to
work it out and that is what matters most.

For Better or for Worse

Everyday I use my tiny hands to squeeze your heart as gently but tightly as I can.
In my mind, I am so cautious about how I handle your heart.
Your heart has slowly become a part of me ever since we met.
I never imagined myself to be with someone like you.
Each battle we've faced has made us stronger and closer.
Each time I pray to the stars for something to change , you try so much harder.

Lonely but Not Alone

I hate being alone and that's something that took me a while to get comfortable saying aloud.

Loneliness has nothing to do with why I still continue to choose you everyday, even when you wonder why.

I've grown with you and you bring out the brightest light inside of me that has been deactivated for so long.

You have opened my eyes to the inauthenticity that I've ignored from other people.

You look out for me in every way possible.

You've brought the feeling of home back into my life.

Be Patient with Me

I wish you didn't have to see me like this.
Puffy eyes and nothing but tears from a stressed mind.
Tears from a wide range of disasters.
Some of these events might not even matter as much as some to
someone else but they matter alot to me.
I am so damaged and I try so hard to not appear that way.

You know that you can't love me in the same way that you've loved
others.
I am different and if I had a solid explanation for all my feelings and
reactions maybe my eyes wouldn't be puffy.
Nothing is perfect and I am grateful for the little things you do for me
and please don't think I'm not.
So for now let me cry and let it all out onto your chest before it
explodes in mines.

Potentially a Supermodel

If there's one thing that you know about me is that I care alot ,
sometimes too much.

You've seen me open myself up to hurt by caring about others who
don't see how much I care about them.

You've seen me on days when I don't feel as beautiful as you think I
am.

You've seen me on days when I feel like the world did a damn good
job of chewing me up and spitting me back out.

However, on these days you see something that I always fail to see.

Strength. Alot of it at that.

Seashells in the Sand
Dancing with seashells around our feet.
The beauty of our souls is so upbeat.
Taking your hand and running where the winds go to
play.
Dreaming of going home with you and forgetting the
rest.

Blue skies and warm breezes is what our love is made of.
Rain clouds are expected and flooding is predicted but
the sun always comes back out to play.
No matter how stormy the weather gets, our love will
survive it.
I hope that every trip I make around the sun allows me
to take you with me.

Black Beauty

Gratitude

Everything I say and everything I do, I will remember all those
black and beautiful people that have come before me.
The people who paved the way so that I can be seen today.
Even though racism and injustice still exists for all the people
that look like me, we have still shown the world that we will not
be played for fools.
I have gratitude in my heart for all the people of colour in my
life who have influenced me in the most positive ways.
I dedicate the next few pages to my beautiful black flowers of all
shapes and sizes. You are important and you are everything.

Being Black on Earth

Wholesome black skin sitting in shade.
Hiding from the enemy who wears a uniform that's tainted
with shame.
Shooting us with guns and damaging our veins with a taser.
We're angry , broken with pain and covered in the blood of
our ancestors.
We can only set fire to rain to demand a wave of change.
I shouldn't have to worry about my life not being seen as equal
because of the melanin on my skin.

Black Woman's Interlude

I hate to fight but sometimes it's all I know.
Being a black woman in this society is a fight within itself
anyways.

My Black Caribbean Girl Anthem

Dark black skin , thick curly hair , plumpy full lips and an island attitude. Going from every creed and race will find an equal place to being silently judged for my blackness. They say they don't understand our accents but they think it's 'cool' to use our slang in every sentence. It's become a 'culture' for others to mimic us and act like they are us. I've seen black women with lots of attitude and driving force.I've seen people criticize it and diminish their strive. But have you considered that we have 'attitude ' because we have been stepped on too many times? Lighter skin doesn't have to struggle with half the things that we do. You can disagree if you want but before you do,take a look back at history and look at your daily life and you would see what I mean. Coming from a land of struggle and spice has taught me alot about life. Things about life that you won't understand. How to appreciate the little things because growing up with less was always more. So yes my attitude is warranted and my thoughts are justified because moving to the 'better' country has made me aware of who I am. My blackness is seen as a threat and sometimes an unattractive view. But no one can be a black woman better than a black woman herself.

So here I am.

Unfiltered.

Real.

Dialect literate.

Full of strength.

So get out of my way if bullshit is the only language you speak.

Appropriation is unwelcomed.

Our Men Cry Too

All men are not the same.

Our men of colour have been defined by stereotypes from the moment they are conceived.

I've met many black men in my life, some were amazing and some weren't as great but they all have one thing in common and that is fear.

The fear of failing, the fear of expressing , the fear of being vulnerable , the fear of being genuine and the fear of the unknown.

For generations; society has made our precious fathers, brothers, husbands, sons, boyfriends and uncles feel like a cry for help is a cry of shame.

There's a gross misconception on what black masculinity needs to look like and this is destroying the men we love in the worst ways.

I've always said to myself that I don't want a son and maybe it's because I'm afraid of what this world might do to him.

If God decides that I am enough to bear a beautiful chocolate boy, me and his father will raise him to express how he feels.

I will remind him every day that the strongest of men are allowed to cry.

Trauma Meets Brown Sugar

No matter how much pain happens within the community somehow our brothers still remain sweet.
Despite seeing the loss of a friend through senseless violence, he still gets an A on his quiz the next day.
He has hopes and dreams but everyday he has to protect his mother from an abusive partner that was abused himself.

The girl of his dreams does not match his skin colour and he does not know how to approach her because her friends think that he is not good enough for her.
Going for a jog at 10 pm sounds amazing but it becomes more complicated when he has to plan his route accordingly so no one will see him.

A young black couple, binded by love and sugar can not open a joint account together without the teller giving looks of judgement.
It is even more embarrassing when they are asked if they are waiting for someone when they were clearly waiting in line to be looked after.
There is so much pain to unravel and not enough time but if we look out for each other, we will be alright.

Joanne

A heart of gold with many smart comebacks.
I had a slight fear of you but it was the good type of fear, the type of
fear that motivated me to always try in everything that I did.
You were with me from the years of seeing the world through
innocent eyes to the years of seeing the world for what it is.
I have had many black female inspirational figures in my life and
you are in the top 3.

From washing my hair to tutoring me ; picking me up from school
when something came up.
Sometimes strict but always reasonable, never sugar coated but
always kissed my tears away.
Running your own business while being super successful in your
career is not something that many people can manage.
There was never a day when you were not busy but you always
made time for me when I needed you.

I could say that I have a godmother who is a superhero that got left
out of the Marvel comics.
She has multiple superpowers and multiple identities.
She is my cousin and godmother all wrapped up in one but she was
more of a mother to me from the first day I met her.
I admired her independence and strong sense of self confidence
for years and I always wished to grow up with these qualities.
She was always improving herself and looking for ways to make
her dreams a reality.
She loves fiercely and when I saw her find love within someone
else it filled me with joy.

Seeing my godmother allow herself to become vulnerable and open up to the man that she married was admirable.
This wasn't easy for someone who is so used to being self sufficient and full of independence.

The vulnerability of this flower helped me to stop being afraid of how hard I love.
This woman sprinkled so much love into me and helped shape me into who I am today.
I'll always love her as fiercely as she loves me.

For a Heart-Broken Black Girl

She was the best thing.
The best thing to walk this earth and the best thing to happen to
you.
Her dark brown skin that reigned supreme in the sunlight and
glowed in the dark.
Glowed in the dark for you under the sheets and she surrendered
her chocolate soul into your unworthy hands.
Her heart is golden and sweet and even when she was mad at you
, her heart still struggled to beat lovingly for you.
I believe that women who do not trust easily are the ones who are
harder to break down but when they let everything go , it is sad
to see the lengths they would go for you.
Almost a decade you stole from her precious life.
Almost a decade of her making you into what you are today.
All the late night drives to be there for you, all the dishes she
served you hot, all the times she put your needs above everyone
else.
Caribbean women in relationships , good and decent ones
especially ones who were raised by the older folks have such a
nurturing nature.
It is embedded in our DNA and it is hard to isolate our good
intentions that we see necessary in order to see the advantage that
is being taken of us.

Her strength is extraordinary and beyond explainable.

Anyone else would have drawn blood for this level of disgrace but God is real and so are demons.

Once you let demons in , it is hard to make them leave.

He threw the treasure of gold into the ocean and picked up a fraudulent piece of silver.

He let another woman take his pure soul and now he is a walking puppet with an ungrateful spirit.

Brown skin girl, you are great and you are my impression because the trials you have been through would have broken me.

You were in a dark place but you found your way out so gracefully and now this is your time to steal all of the shine.

Growing With Time

95

Hope for the Hopeless

Feeling comfort in knowing that you are here after fighting
hard and long is one of the best feelings in this lifetime.
A sense of gratitude for the many connections that positively
contributed to your life.
A moment of silence for the leaves that didn't get enough of
the evening showers.
Let's believe that the sun would make up for it tomorrow.

Reflections

As the sun comes up, they look back at what once was.
They look back at how they got here and what made them.
We look at the happy, the fears, the pains, the mistakes,
the regrets, the losses and the wins that make up our
stories.
My only wish is that when we are called home at sunset;
we have learnt by then.

You Will Get There

Getting out of bed won't be easy because the comfort of your sheets will never betray you.
There will be bad days where you wouldn't even want to look in the mirror to wash your face and start your day.
You will feel like you can't breathe in social settings and you will hold your breathe ; hoping no one would notice.

Something would remind you of your pain and you will feel like you can never overcome it.
The process of becoming whole again is not like a warm bed on a cold winter night or a soft chocolate chip cookie at midnight.
Becoming whole again means digging deeper inside yourself and unpacking your pain.

It won't be easy but in the end you will be able to breathe and be content with how far you have come and how far you are willing to go.
While unpacking your pain, you will uncover who you truly are inside.
Someone who is strong and wants to survive each day with a smile.

A Prayer

Maybe not today.
Maybe not even tomorrow however one day God will show me
that the way I am is a blessing in disguise.
The way I think will make the sidewalks turn from gray to gold.

The way I love will help flowers find relief while sweating in the
blazing sun.
The way I work will secure a prosperous future once I have faith.
Maybe not today and not even tomorrow but on another day I will
not apologize for what I am or doubt what I'm going to be.

Slow but Sure Recovery

As the days grow longer and the nights grow shorter , I have learnt that time and patience can indeed heal wounds.

Always Worthy

The way you love me has given me warmth in my heart and more confidence in myself.

The way you look at me has given me energy to wake up on days when I don't want to.

You loving me has reminded me that I was always worthy.

The ones before you just weren't worthy of the love I had to give.

The F Word

Forgiveness is difficult for me.

I don't always forgive myself and I struggle immensely to forgive others.

Forgiving others is never a favor that you're doing for the other person and forgiving yourself is a favor you're doing for you.

Maybe my problem is that I don't love myself enough to not hold a grudge.

It's not that I want to , I assure you I try.

This is a process for me and I am willing to take it one step at a time.

If Maturity Could Speak

Being mature means owning up to your mistakes and taking
responsibility for your actions.
Recognizing that sometimes we aren't our best selves in every moment
means that we are growing.

Be mindful of how others feel when they are around you.
Be mindful of how you make them feel when they are around you.
Don't expect people to accept your selfish or ignorant ways.
Because at the end of the day that isn't who you are.
It's just a habit to be unlearned.

Stop investing your time and feelings into people who exploit you.
The truth is hard to process but it's necessary to save yourself from
unnecessary pain.
Some people can change but some people are not willing to.
When you start to appreciate yourself more, you will begin to see who is
worthy of your time energy.

Let's Be Honest

Sometimes hearing the truth is like a loud and annoying sound
and it's always the hardest to swallow and digest.
Some of us never like to be wrong or think that there isn't
anything wrong with some of our actions.
We don't think about the consequences , we just act.

We like to live in the moment without thinking about our
future.
We take offense to the concerns of our actions and dismiss it as
negative vibes.
We all do it... don't deny it.
However, if someone never tells you the truth then they never
cared about you to begin with.
I learnt that the hard way and I'm sure you did too.

No Answers

There's a lot of answers that I don't have.
That's life and I found that out with a tumble and a fall.
I came crashing down on my face and I never thought I was going to recover.
The emotions I felt were unbearable and excruciating but I choose to get up and brush myself off.
I choose to look in the mirror and slowly learn how to not beat myself up as much as before.
All I know is that, soon enough, I won't be afraid to bloom once again.

Healing The Branches

Self-Loveliness

Self-love is such a complicated thing.
Or maybe I make it complicated by listening to everything that I am
not.
Instead of loving everything that I know I am.

How it Hurts

When I am hurt, it takes me a long time to truly get over what hurt me.

My thoughts become crippled by my hurt and it thinks about revenge.

It took me a long time to realize that I am only hurting myself more by letting my hurt devour me.

However I refuse to ignore my pain and pretend like it withered away.

I will sit with my pain and understand it.

I will take it for some fresh air and then I will tell my pain to move on.

It won't happen overnight but as long as my pain knows that I don't want to be in pain anymore; it will wither away.

Dreams

Beyond these gray skies and lonely nights there must be some kind of sunshine and company that allows me to be everything and anything that I want to be.
For now , I will count all the stars at night.
With hopes that I could shine just like them on all nights.

It's Time to Believe

The hurt will never stop.
Unless we choose to let go.
The hurt will never stop if we don't forgive ourselves and allow
our hearts to love.

To let go of old love and embrace what is ahead is sometimes
scarier than anything under your bed.
Just breathe and know that you can't make a conclusion based
on something that hasn't played out yet.
Someone is ready and willing to love you for all you are so just
let it flow.

Truthfully

I will admit that I try to seek the bad in every situation.
I do because I hate disappointment and avoidable circumstances.
I hate not knowing if I can trust someone or not, even if they seem like the
nicest person ever.
It's hard to not push what I think is right for someone else and maybe this is
because I grew up so barricaded from things that were meant to teach me
something.

Sometimes I'm seen as a controlling person because some people are more
headstrong than others and I am too resilient to let go.
Resilience is good when you keep trying but it isn't good when you push
others who aren't ready yet.
I love very hard and care about others with every inch of my heart.
Sometimes my love can be suffocating.
Suffocating to the point where people might retreat.

My fear of losing people is bigger than me.
People lose people everyday but for me; it's like the sky is falling.
I care too much to give people space to grow in their own ways.
I am slowly using everything that I see is wrong with me in a way that
doesn't hinder the loving soul that is within me.

What Does Healing Mean To You?

Healing is spreading yourself thin and being able to recover by admitting to yourself that you really did s p r e a d yourself t h i n.

Special

You are you and no one else can be like you, think like you, talk like you or look like you.

You are competing against your reflection and no one else is in this race with you.

Believe that no one can come close to your potential.

Know that no one else can take away what was meant for you.

Come so Far

You have seen the earth and the moon fight among themselves.
You have seen the ocean fight with the earth's anger and take it out
on everything in its path.
Disappointment has knocked on your door and offered you half-
dead flowers.
Despite it all you still woke up every morning and believed that
something would change.
Even if the change was small; you embraced it with so much love.
You tried each day to improve every part of you and this will never
go unrewarded.
So please keep going because I am proud of you.